# GET a
# GRIP

# GET a GRIP

## Turning Better *into* Best
## & Adversity *into* Success

# Al Horner

BRONZE BOW PUBLISHING
MINNEAPOLIS, MINNESOTA

*This book is
dedicated to*
**DIANE.**
*It is also
dedicated to all
who willingly face
tough decisions
for the benefit of
others.*

# CONTENTS

# FOREWORD

We all have gifts. One of my gifts is fixing messes. For over thirty years I've walked into difficult situations, figured out what needs to be done and then done it well enough so the messes became successes. An important part of my problem solving process is The Checklist described in this book.

During those years I've also seen friends and acquaintances struggle or fail in various situations. Frequently these folks could not see the critical problem that was causing the difficulty. If they had understood and used The Checklist it would have been a shortcut to success. So I resolved to put The Checklist into a form that others could use, hoping to give folks a tool that would provide help when help was needed. When things are difficult you don't need more complexity, so this book is short, simple, and direct.

I keep The Checklist near my desk. When I'm confused it helps me see solutions. When things are going well, it helps me make things even better.

I offer this book to you hoping The Checklist will guide you to more success and happiness whether you are in good times or bad.

# CHAPTER ONE

# "What Should I Do?"

The airliner cabin is quiet and the hypnotic rhythm of the engines lulls you to sleep. You're looking forward to a smooth flight as the jet soars through 35,000 feet. But in the cockpit, a red warning light suddenly flashes.

"Oh no!" The pilot's brow furrows and his eyes squint at the light. "This is not good." He takes a deep breath and begins his emergency checklist. Halfway through the list, he figures out the problem's cause. Then he takes corrective action, and the light flickers off. The problem is solved while you sleep. Life is good.

On another day your loved one is driving home as a downpour drenches the highway. During those first rainy moments, road oil and water mix to form a treacherous slick, and there is a crunching car accident. In the emergency room, the trauma surgeon shifts into high gear. With professional detachment acquired through years of practice, she moves through her checklist, determining the type and extent of your loved one's injuries. Based on that quick assessment, she treats the problems. A few days later, the trauma is past and complete recovery is expected. Life will soon be good again.

We trust pilots and doctors with our lives and the lives of those we love. When trouble strikes, these professionals don't have time to call specialists or consultants, so they use proven checklists to identify problems quickly. Then they take action to avoid disaster.

## GET A GRIP

> *As a young SEAL officer, I learned the power of checklists when a grizzled old Master Chief got in my face and offered some forceful advice. He said, "Mr. Horner, listen to me. I SAY AGAIN—LISTEN TO ME! You better learn about the 7 P's: Proper Prior Planning Prevents Pathetically Poor Performance. Pay attention to that so no one gets hurt."*

It was one of those priceless moments when years of experience speak to youthful overconfidence. In the SEAL Teams we frequently faced life-and-death situations and had precious little time to make critical decisions. Part of what the Chief was telling me was to use checklists so I wouldn't make painful mistakes that others had already learned how to avoid. We survived, and the Chief gets at least part of the credit.

You don't have to be a pilot, surgeon, or SEAL to face tough moments where it's essential that you get a grip on the situation quickly and take action. Whether in your personal life or career, you've had brain-pain, stomach-tightening situations in the past, and you'll have more of them in the future unless you move into a closet and lock the door. But even then, sooner or later, you'll have to decide when to come out. Tough decisions are a wonderful part of life; they lead to growth. But if there's no expert to help you, how will you react when the question looms: "What should I do?"

Simplistically, you have two choices. First, you can wing it, letting your emotions and thoughts interact until you feel an answer that seems right. This intuitive process can produce good answers, but is that how you would have wanted the pilot and the surgeon to approach the critical moments they faced? Your second choice is to do what professionals do and use a checklist to structure your thinking.

Whether you're considering a personal challenge, facing a tough financial decision, or trying to solve a business organizational problem, your choices remain the same—wing it...or use a checklist that is based upon wisdom from successful past experience to guide you to right actions. The discipline of using a checklist stacks the odds in your favor and is the wise way to proceed in most difficult situations.

Effective troubleshooting checklists are short and simple. In times of stress, simpler is better. The Checklist I developed during my SEAL years can be completed quickly because speed and simplicity were built into it. It helped me see clearly through tough situations on very dark nights.

Over the past 30 years I have refined The Checklist and used it to turn around six failing businesses in different industries—service, manufacturing, construction, retail, and wholesale—with a perfect win/loss ratio of 6/0. It also helped me guide several non-profit organizations through trying times. One win could be called luck and two wins could be called lots of luck. But after several consecutive wins in diverse situations, it has to be more than luck. In each of the businesses and non-profits, I knew little about the market or competitive circumstances, but The Checklist helped me figure out where the biggest problems were so we solved them first, and we succeeded every time.

During these years I also faced the typical challenges of a husband, father, and friend. At each difficult decision point, The Checklist helped me. Using it became a winning habit.

## THE VALUE OF A CHECKLIST

> *You're facing a person who is not breathing, has broken bones, and serious cuts. What do you do? CPR offers a clear checklist process to make certain you do the right thing first. Before you fix broken bones or treat cuts, the checklist instructs you to restore breathing. If you follow the procedure, you can save the person's life. If you don't, you may lose the victim despite your valiant efforts. Following the checklist is essential for success.*

The Checklist stays on my desk so it's accessible. If I'm confused, it helps me sort out the issues, visualize a plan, and work on the right priorities. Even when things are going well, a periodic Checklist review always highlights something that needs to be done better. This small time investment yields a good return.

You don't have to be someone special to use The Checklist successfully. You just have to be honest with yourself. There are five basic Checklist questions. Each explores a topic that's critical to successful completion of any task. To use The Checklist you simply ask yourself the first question and answer "Yes," "No," or "I'm not sure."

"Yes" means you have no problem with that issue and can move on to the next checkpoint."

No" means you have identified an issue that needs attention. Stop what you're doing, because whatever you are considering is not going to work until you solve a problem in that topic area. "No" means there is a crack in the foundation, a weak link in the chain, an ingredient missing in the recipe. Sooner or later that issue will create a significant problem unless it is fixed. It may be the reason you're wrestling with a problem or issue right now.

"I don't know" means you need to consider the checkpoint in more depth to get to a "Yes" or "No."

Problems fall into general groups. Teachers, coaches, team leaders, managers, politicians, and everyone else who makes important decisions face the same generic problems—they just come in packages with different wrappers. As you read each chapter, you'll find general solutions for each group of general problems. You can adapt the general solutions to your specific situation.

You will also find Pearls. In the SEAL Teams, older, more experienced men sometimes told us young guys they were giving us a Pearl. That meant, "Pay attention because someone got hurt learning this lesson for us." The Pearls in the chapters are pieces of wisdom that will save you pain.

## PEARLS

In Combat Swimmers School we learned how to dive using pure oxygen, nitrogen/oxygen mixes, and compressed air. The training covered decompression tables, underwater navigation, and tons of information about equipment.

One day a veteran told us he was giving us a Pearl. He paused to get our complete attention and then said, "Exhale on the way up."

Being a cocky young stud, I almost blew right past that little gem. But the message soon became significant. He was saying that if you're in an emergency and you forget everything you know about diving, remember one thing—exhale as you swim to the surface. The reason, as all experienced divers know, is that if you don't exhale on the way up you can explode your lungs and you may die. He took very complex information and sorted it down to one critical, lifesaving point that people had learned from painful lessons. That's a Pearl.

Pearls are waiting for you throughout this book to guide

you in places that may seem complicated and need simplicity for clarity. They are simply beautiful.

The value of The Checklist and the Pearls is that they will help you sort through complex situations so you can determine what's most important. If you're in a difficult spot, you must identify the most critical problem and focus on it rather than something else. An elegant, skillfully executed solution that solves the wrong problem is useless. You'll have solved *a* problem, but it won't matter if the plane crashes or the patient dies. Use The Checklist to identify and resolve *the key* problem first.

Chapter 2 has a short version of The Checklist. After you've used The Checklist a few times, this is all you'll need. But your first times through it, you'll want to read about each checkpoint in the designated chapters. These chapters explain each checkpoint and will help you understand the checkpoint question so you can answer it knowledgeably and honestly. If you are unclear about what a checkpoint question really means, go to its chapter for background information and illustrative anecdotes.

Chapter 8 has several real-world examples using The Checklist. The examples are from different scenarios and demonstrate how simple and effective the checklist process can be.

When you're wrestling with an important problem,

there is only one wise thing to do—use a checklist based upon wisdom from past experience to stack the odds in your favor.

If you have a better checklist, use it. If you don't, enjoy mine. It works!

## PEARL #1

THE 7 P's:

**P**roper

**P**rior

**P**lanning

**P**revents

**P**athetically

**P**oor

**P**erformance.

This is a version of "A stitch in time saves nine" and "An ounce of prevention is worth a pound of cure." The message is clear, and The Checklist will help you put structure in your problem solving.

# CHAPTER TWO

# The Quick Checklist

Think about the problem you're trying to solve or the question you're trying to answer. The more clearly you define the problem or question, the clearer the answers will be. Take out a pad of paper and write down the problem or question, because writing it increases clarity and sharpens focus. Examples include:

"What's the problem with (*my team, our organization, my group*)?"

"Should I accept responsibility to (*start the project, lead the effort, fix the problem*)?"

"Should I get involved with (*this company, this charity, this project*)?"

"Should I invest in (*this business, this project, this group*)?"

"Why isn't (*my group, my team, my company*) working?"

"Why is (*my business, my team, my charity*) losing money?"

First, define the problem or question, then go through the questions in The Checklist below and answer each one. For each checkpoint think about the question carefully, then honestly answer "Yes" or "No." Write your answers in pencil so you can use The Quick Checklist for future questions.

|  | Yes | No |
|---|---|---|
| Checkpoint **1**: Is my/our commitment level strong enough? | | |
| • Time | ___ | ___ |
| • Money | ___ | ___ |
| • Emotional energy | ___ | ___ |
| Checkpoint **2**: Is my/our vision a clear winner? | ___ | ___ |
| • Who are the customers? | | |
| • What do they value most? | | |
| • How do we provide differentiated value? | | |
| • How do we sustain ourselves? | | |
| Checkpoint **3**: Is the team a clear winner? | ___ | ___ |
| Checkpoint **4**: Will the leaders handle crises well? | ___ | ___ |
| Checkpoint **5**: Will my loved ones get what they need? | ___ | ___ |

If you answered "Yes" to each question, then you either have no problems to overcome or you haven't answered the questions knowledgeably and honestly.

If you answered "No" to any question, that's a red light, and you have defined an area that needs attention. If you have more than one "No," you have multiple problems to solve. Solve them in order, first one first, second one second. The sequence of The Checklist questions is important because each checkpoint builds on the previous one.

If you're uncertain whether your answer is "Yes" or "No" to any question, that's a yellow light. Proceed with caution. Go to the chapter that explains the checkpoint and read the material. As you think about the topic and read the anecdotes, the yellow light will turn green or red, "Yes" or "No." If you answer "Yes," proceed to the next checkpoint. If you answer "No," look for general solutions in the chapter.

If you want to read about real-life cases of how The Checklist has worked in various scenarios, Chapter 8 presents several examples.

# CHAPTER THREE

# Commitment

## CHECKPOINT #1:

### "Is My/Our Commitment Strong Enough?"

In this checkpoint, you have to imagine the future…visualize it, live it as vividly as you can. And while you're doing it, answer the checkpoint question honestly. It's easy to bias your perspective and view the future unrealistically through rose-colored glasses. Take off the glasses or you'll set yourself up for trouble.

Keep this principle in mind: Any significant task will consume more time, money, and energy than you expect. Therefore, you will face more challenges than you anticipate at the front end. You must factor this into your answers.

If your commitment is stronger than the challenges, you can succeed. If it isn't, you'll fail.

## HOW MUCH COMMITMENT IS REQUIRED?

We've all heard about the power of commitment in sayings and adages since we were young. "It's not over until the fat lady sings." "It's not over until it's over." "Many people are stronger, many are smarter...but perseverance wins" (Vince Lombardi abridged). But hearing about commitment does not mean we understand it.

There are two subtle points related to commitment. The first point is that we usually underestimate how much commitment will be required to complete a tough task. Have you ever invested in an enterprise where the first financial commitment was the last? Have you ever started a serious project that took less time than you expected? Ever begun a tough task that required less emotional energy than you expected? Unless you're very lucky, whatever you're considering will take more commitment than you expect.

If your beginning commitment level is shaky, you're likely to fail. But if you're absolutely committed, you can win even against overwhelming odds. The following two stories illustrate how strong commitment leads to success.

## HELL WEEK—THE NIGHT RUN

*Hell Week in BUD/S (Basic UDT/SEAL Training) is*

legendary as the toughest military training in the free world. The rigors of this training have been thoroughly documented on television in recent years. The first time I really understood the meaning of "commitment" was during my long night run in Hell Week.

Our group started in the dark at the end of the third long day. In the previous three days we had slept a little over an hour, spending our days and nights doing hard physical training in a cold February Chesapeake Bay drizzle. The air and water temperatures were in the high forties, and our salty, wet cotton fatigues provided no warmth. This particular version of Hell was cold, and I was so hungry that my shoe looked like a potential hors d'ouvre.

Our instructors ran us to the beach, and we began to struggle mile after mile through the soft sand. I was the best swimmer in our class, but I wasn't a strong runner. My biggest fear was that I would crumble during the eighteen-mile night run. Then they decided that the sand dunes looked interesting, so we ran up and down them for an hour. Guys were quitting all around me...it was over for them.

I used every trick I knew to keep going. I imagined being weightless and floating over the sand—that didn't last long. I took my mind to a warm sunny place while my body kept running—that didn't last long either. Sometimes I fell in next to a classmate, and we helped each other by synchronizing our steps. Then my legs started to cramp. I focused on running loose—keeping my leg muscles relaxed—but they were ready to knot up.

As I plodded through thick brush on the edge of the beach, one of the instructors stopped and lay down across my path. I had to either go through the brush around him or jump over him. In a testosterone-induced flash of defiance, I jumped over him. Bad choice! My trailing foot nicked him, and he dropped me for a hundred push-ups.

Just prior to Hell Week this would have been no problem, but at this point it was a big deal. After 50 push-ups, I was weak. After 75, I was shaking. When I got to 100, I felt as though my body had given up all its energy to my arms, where it had drained through my fingertips into the sand. I willed it back, but it wouldn't come. As I collapsed on the path, I couldn't see my classmates, and the instructor looked down at me.

"There's no way you can catch those guys," he sneered. Then he pointed to a van close by that had food, water, hot coffee, and blankets. "Why not be done with all the pain and cold. Let's get some hot coffee."

For the first time I doubted my ability to continue. My body was numb, and I wasn't sure how I could walk one hundred yards let alone run for hours more. I don't know how long it took, probably only a few seconds, but I thought about how long I'd dreamed of being a SEAL, how much I wanted to wear the Trident on my chest, the pain I'd already gone through to get to this point, and how ashamed I'd feel if I quit. I gave myself no choice except to continue.

"I won't quit!" I spat back at him. Looking down the path, I decided that I could take a couple more steps. I whispered "Hooyah" to myself, stood, and took a step down the path.

In a quiet voice behind me, I heard the instructor say, "Good choice, Mr. Horner." I was surprised, but it felt good.

Immediately all concept of time vanished. I don't remember the next couple of hours as the darkness and my tunnel vision shut out everything around me. I focused on getting one foot in front of the other. Finally dawn's first light touched the horizon and the run was over.

Our class started with 73 men and only 13 remained after this week.

Commitment isn't just about tough guys. Women make steel-hard commitments, too.

## DANCING DIANE

*Diane loved dancing. She began lessons at age three, and at age four she performed for the national dance master's convention. Though her parents stopped her lessons at age ten, she still loved dancing. After graduating from college, she became a music teacher, wife, and mother. Her life was good, but deep inside she knew she was really a dancer.*

*At age twenty-eight she began teaching dance-exercise classes. Women loved the freedom and joy of dancing with her; it became an emotionally vital part of their week. They would tell Diane about a new favorite song, and she would choreograph a routine for it. Then they'd all dance the new routine together, lost in the music, movements, and freedom. She loved giving them the gift of dance.*

*To reach more people, Diane decided to make commercial videos. During a year of creative effort, she spent endless hours and thousands of dollars producing a demonstration tape. Her friends helped her frequently. She spent another year pitching sponsors, producers, and distributors—and getting rejected. The process was frustrating and difficult as she tried to balance it with a family and job, but she persevered. Finally she quit her job to work full time on the project.*

A month later the Achy-Breaky line dance craze started. A video distributor asked if she could quickly make an instructional tape of hot country line dances to catch the front end of the new fad. She agreed. Shooting was scheduled to begin in three days. Diane had to create instructional music (there was no time to get rights to existing music), recruit dancers, put together costumes, decide how to format the instruction, and create a script. One-by-one she completed the tasks with the help of her friends.

Despite the short lead time, her video was a huge success. It outsold all competing products and stayed on the Billboard Top 40 list for 45 weeks. The videos sold over 2.7 million copies, becoming the best-selling special interest video series ever released. During 1992 to 1994, Diane appeared frequently on television and at promotional events throughout North America. Everyone recognized her as "that dance lady," Dancing Diane.

> "WINNING ISN'T EVERYTHING BUT WANTING TO IS."
> —Vince Lombardi

The road to success was long and bumpy, but my wife stayed committed to her dream and it came true.

## MANAGING YOUR COMMITMENT LEVEL

The second subtle point regarding commitment is that it is not stable. You have the power to make strong commitments weaker and weak commitments stronger. Whether you are at the beginning of a task and need help getting started or in the middle of a task and need a boost, here are five techniques to help manage your commitment level:

*1. When You're Unsure About the Strength of Your Commitment...Live the Outcome in Your Imagination.*
Visualize the outcome and experience it in living color. How does it feel? How much time will it take? How much money will it consume? How will it affect those you love? The more clearly you imagine it, the more clearly you'll know if your commitment is strong enough to achieve it.

If you don't like the feeling "Congratulations," you're lucky to see it now. Terminating an unattractive pursuit at the front end seems wise. Terminating the pursuit after you and others have a significant time, money, or emotional investment seems like quitting.

But, if you like the feeling, your commitment will increase.

> *When I was lying on the sand during the night run trying to decide if I was going to quit or continue, I visualized myself wearing the SEAL badge on my chest. It felt good, and I was proud I had earned it. I knew right then that being tired and cold wasn't going*

to stop me. *They'd have to break my leg to keep me from continuing the run.*

*2. When You're Afraid…Know That Courage Trumps Fear.*
Fear is a state of being—you're either afraid or you're not. Saying "Don't be afraid" is like saying "Don't be six feet tall." It's not a choice. You either are afraid or you aren't, and everyone is afraid of something. But whether you're afraid or not isn't what matters. The key is your willingness to be courageous.

> **"COURAGE IS MASTERY OF FEAR, NOT ABSENCE OF FEAR."** —Mark Twain

You miss 100 percent of the shots you don't take. If you want something, you've got to take a chance. Fear is normal when you face a challenge, and you can't make fear just go away. But generating enough courage to take the first step can launch you. It's like facing fear in the airplane door when you first skydive. Once you've gathered enough courage to take the first step, you're on your way.

The bravest acts are those done by people who understand what they are about to do, are afraid, and then muster enough courage to take action. Courage is the key.

*As Diane's videos became a hit, her distributor scheduled her on national TV, The Vicky (Lawrence) Show, for a promotional appearance with several country music stars. She was scared stiff as she flew to Los Angeles, was picked up by the studio limo, and was escorted to a preparation room next to Johnny Carson's.*

*Her mind screamed, "What am I doing here!" as she looked around and realized that millions of people were about to watch her and she was going to be onstage with stars. She knew that her distributor and the whole sales team were counting on her to perform well, and all the friends who supported her would be watching the show. She could barely breathe. But when the moment arrived, she pulled together all her courage and forced herself to walk out on the stage—she was irreversibly committed at that point.*

Summon the courage to take the first step.

*3. When the Going Gets a Little Tough…*
*Support Can Get You Through.*
You can receive support from many sources.

*During Hell Week, we gave each other support at critical times, synchronizing our running steps or offering words of encouragement. A simple joke buoyed our spirits; a helping hand showed that someone cared; and even the instructor's quiet, "Good choice, Mr. Horner," during the night run gave me a boost.*

*When Diane was going through years of rejection, her friends encouraged her. And when she had three days to do three-weeks worth of preparation to shoot the first video, her friends rallied for her again. Whenever she was sinking, she accepted energy from others that buoyed her up.*

If you understand anything about recovering from chemical dependency and participating in AA, you understand the incredible power of support. POWs have received sustaining energy from the briefest of contacts with fellow prisoners. People of faith have access to an immense reservoir of energy. Support groups are available in many shapes and sizes if you just open yourself to them and ask for a little help. There are people who care about you. Identify where your sources of support are and plug into them when your battery runs low. It's the right thing for you to do, and it's right to encourage others who need a little help.

When you're in the middle of a tough situation and hitting overload, support is always available. Just be open to accepting it, ask for it, and you can receive it.

*4. When the Going Gets Really Tough…*
*Take One Bite-Size Step at a Time.*
When you're feeling overwhelmed at the size or complexity of the whole task, break the job into small steps. Figure

out what the next bite-size piece is and do it. You'll get that small action done and make a little progress. That progress will energize you to take the next step and you'll make more progress.

> Late in Hell Week there were times when I didn't know how much more I could take, and it scared me. In those moments I stopped thinking about how much more we had to do and just focused on the next step. I didn't know if I could make it all week, didn't know if I could make it through the day, and wasn't sure if I could make it through the hour. But I knew I could take one more step. By breaking the whole scary task into small enough pieces, I got it done.
>
> Diane faced the seemingly impossible task of creating a concept for her video; getting music, dancers, and costumes ready; creating her script; obtaining a shooting location; and creating a set…all in three days. It was overwhelming. To get through it she organized the tasks and completed them one piece at a time.

All tasks are nothing more than a series of small actions. If you break the daunting task down into a series of small steps and move through them one at a time, you can complete the task. If any of the small actions seems too difficult, break it down into even smaller pieces, and you can make progress. String these pieces together and you succeed.

5. *When Doubts Are Creeping In...Self-Talk Buoys You Up or Drags You Down.*

Self-talk is that continuous internal conversation you have with yourself. Whether you are conscious of it or not, you do it day and night. When you become conscious of it and take control of it, you can direct your self-talk so that you feel better or worse.

A gentle rain...sometimes it's beautiful and sometimes it's miserable. One day it's soothing and the next it's gloomy. At one time or another you've probably talked yourself into both feelings. You have a choice about how to perceive it. When you take control of your self-talk, you're in charge and no longer a victim.

The great thing about understanding self-talk is knowing that you can control it. By managing your self-talk, you can bring in the sunshine or stir up a storm. You have the power—the choice is yours.

> *In the last hours of Hell Week, I was so weak and delusional I could barely move. But the other guys were in the same condition. I said to myself, "I won't quit until after all of them do." I was talking myself into winning. It worked.*

*Diane kept her vision alive through the bad times by saying to herself, "I love dancing, and I love giving that feeling to others." She focused on her joy and the joy of those who danced with her. She was unstoppable.*

## PEARL #2

**WHOEVER GIVES UP FIRST LOSES**

Small cats beat large dogs. David beat Goliath. One person can inspire and lead millions of people. The message is clear: "It's not the size of the critter in the fight; it's the size of fight in the critter!"

## SUMMARY

If you've figured out that your commitment level is not strong enough, congratulations! You've just saved yourself time, money, or emotional pain, because now you know there is no need to proceed.

If you're unsure whether your commitment level is strong enough and you want to proceed, then understand that you have a commitment problem and use the five techniques to manage your commitment level.

## WHAT'S NEXT?

If your commitment is strong enough, it's time to build the foundation. Go to checkpoint #2.

# CHAPTER FOUR

# Vision

## CHECKPOINT #2: "Is My/Our Vision a Clear Winner?"

This is the most complicated checkpoint because the question has four parts and you face a tough adversary...your ego. It's easy to think the answers are obvious and self-evident, but that's a mistake. Flawed vision is the largest cause of failures.

As with the Commitment checkpoint, it's easy to deceive yourself here. You will be planting the seeds of failure if you gloss over the following four questions and answer them superficially or dishonestly.

If you go through all the other checkpoints and don't have a clear answer to your question or problem, then come back here because you probably missed something in the Vision checkpoint. Consider the four questions carefully.

## THE FOUR VISION QUESTIONS

1. Who are you serving?
2. What do those whom you serve value most?
3. How do you provide the value in a differentiated way?
4. How will you sustain the effort financially?

If the problem you are wrestling with is a personal issue, then substitute yourself wherever I talk about an organization. For example, if you are struggling with whether or not to take on a new challenge, the questions become: "What do I value most?" "Which choice will provide me the most value?" "How will this affect me financially?"

## SUCCESSFUL VISIONS

Only disciplined thought can yield a strong vision. It's the principle of garbage in, garbage out. If you skimp on creating your vision, you'll generate trash.

Planning and revising plans require the best minds you can assemble. Ideally, these minds have been there, done that, and won in matters directly related to what you are planning. The strength of the plan will correlate directly with the strength and experience of the minds that create it.

Ego is your enemy here, and it can hurt you three ways.

*Ego Trap #1: I Can Create My Vision Alone.* This big mistake gets made all too often. I've never seen two experienced, committed, intelligent people produce a worse idea than one person can. You are shortchanging yourself or those who count on you if you don't involve the best minds available. And valuable, breakthrough ideas typically originate from good people who are new to the team and not vested in preserving the status quo. If these people understand the objective, they will approach it using experiences you don't have. Multiple perspectives from successful people will always provide you better ideas than you will create alone. In the end, the vision must be yours, but make it strong by gathering wise input from smart, successful people.

> **"NO MAN IS SMART ENOUGH BY HIMSELF."**
> —Plautus

*Ego Trap #2: I Know What My Customers Value.* What you think your customers value is irrelevant. Get your ego out of the way. Don't be a focus group of one. The only perspective that matters is the customer's. It's easy to presume your experience gives you great insight, but change is happening at an accelerating pace. Technology, competitive innovations, materials, systems, and foreign competition are all affecting your customers in ways you cannot understand without continuously listening to them. Having a clear understanding of your customers' needs is an advantage today, but it can be a disadvantage tomorrow unless you continuously revise it in response to the changes affecting your customers.

*Ego Trap #3: My Plan Is Rock Solid.* You need to understand that your plan from yesterday is probably wrong today. You can stamp "wrong" on all plans that have not been revised *very* recently. Conditions are changing continuously, and plans need revision as they are executed. If your ego-attachment to the plan won't let you see changing conditions and make revisions, you are hurting yourself and those who count on you. This is true for battle plans, business plans, sales plans, and personal plans. Sticking with an outdated plan leads to pain; revisioning is always necessary because change is constant. And the pace of change is quickening.

## TRENDS TO DEAL WITH

During the 1980s and 1990s, when our economy was expanding every year, the challenge was to optimize growth. Since 9/11, the challenge is to survive in new circumstances that include the following trends:

*Commoditization.* In the '80s and '90s, mass customization was a buzzword, but now it's simpler. The scope of customization has been reduced; fewer elements of any product or service are being changed. The pressure to decrease costs and shorten lead times is driving products and services toward commoditization. That means that goods and services are being standardized to the greatest extent possible, and customization is being limited to only those features that are most critical to the user. A reality that is driving this is the increased use of low cost foreign labor.

If your vision doesn't include commoditization, it is outdated already.

*Foreign Sourcing.* Any product with high labor content that is a standardized product or has a production lead time greater than a month or two is appropriate for production offshore. In the 1990s, migration of this type of production was to Mexico, Korea, and Indonesia. In the early 2000s China is the logical place to produce these products, because of incredibly low costs and consistent quality.

Telephone service centers and document processing have moved outside the U.S. in huge numbers. With inexpensive communication technology, it only makes sense to hire someone in India to answer the phone at a small fraction of the U.S. cost. In the 1990s, these jobs migrated from U.S. metropolitan areas to lower cost call centers in the Midwest and southeastern states; now these services have migrated offshore.

If your vision doesn't embrace foreign sourcing, it is vulnerable because your costs are likely to be higher than your competitors' costs.

*Instantaneous Communication.* Whether you are processing

student applications, orders for products, customer inquiries, or engineering drawings, the new standard is lightning fast communication. People are not willing to wait for answers or information, and if you force them to wait, they'll probably go elsewhere rather than accept the delay.

If your vision doesn't provide for instantaneous communication, it is obsolete.

These three trends are only a few of the parameters influencing change today. Tomorrow other factors will emerge, creating an endlessly morphing environment. Your need for revisioning never ends, but you can stay current by continuously keeping the four vision questions in front of you.

## 1. WHO ARE YOU SERVING?

Very few people serve only one customer group. If you sell through a distribution system, you must meet the needs of each distribution layer, and the needs of each layer are unique. This reality becomes even more complex if you sell to multiple customer groups through different distribution systems, because you have many customer groups, each with unique needs.

*Example 1—a New Product.* If your product or service is not selling well, you're not meeting the needs of at least one group.

*Three men had twenty years of experience selling to homeowners, and based on their experience they believed their customers would love their new doorframe. After spending several hundred thousand dollars on design, engineering, product development, and patent applications, they were ready to market it. They were so confident that their leader often said, "This is so good we can send in a dog with a note and we'll get an order."*

*Unfortunately, dogs don't sell the product; it's sold through distributors. When it was offered to distributors, nothing happened. After a year of frustration, the team realized that distributors had needs for training and sales support materials that the men had not addressed. The planning effort had focused solely on the needs of end-users—residential homeowners—and had not considered the needs of those in the distribution chain between manufacturing and the end-users.*

*By the time the boys realized why sales weren't happening, they were out of money and enthusiasm. Their vision failed to recognize the unique needs of distributors in their selling chain, and that failure killed the product because it never got through the distributors to the homeowners.*

*Example 2—a Philanthropic Effort.* If you are in a non-profit, charity, or church, you have at least two sets of customers—those whom you serve and those who give you money. These two groups are different; be certain you know exactly what each group needs.

Many third world economies have no social security or welfare system and fail to provide for widows. This tragic situation creates immense suffering for these women and their children. Though there is no bureaucratic structure to assist them, these women are highly motivated to provide for their families.

A group of smart, well-intentioned people studied this harsh reality and devised a concept to help these women. They formed a U.S. non-profit company and funded a foreign business that made micro-loans ($50 to $1000) to groups of these women. The women cross-guaranteed one another's loans, so if one woman defaulted in her payments, the other women covered that woman's payments. Loan losses were almost nonexistent, and the women provided a wonderful support network for one another. The women's small businesses—providing shirts, baked goods, and an incredible variety of other products and services—brought these families from starvation to comparative comfort and many heartwarming stories unfolded.

But the local organization that coordinated the loan program was unstable and instances of fraud and theft *of funds occurred. Though donors who provided funds to the program believed in the good that was being done, they couldn't tolerate contributing to the greed of the local administrators. The operation was excellent at meeting the needs of the women and children they wanted to help, but failed to meet the accountability needs of the donors. Donations decreased, the program struggled, and families went hungry until the needs of the donors were met through reorganization of the foreign business.*

If you are part of a competitive sports team, you have several sets of customers—the fans, the players, and the owners. Each of these groups has different needs. Fans need entertainment and a winning record; players need compensation and fair treatment, and owners need a financial and emotional return on their investment. If any group doesn't get what they need, the team will struggle or fail.

If you are a teacher, you must meet the needs of your students, their parents, and your organization. Students and parents want high quality education; the administration wants compliance with its policies and budgets. Both sets of needs must be met for a teacher to function successfully.

If you are in government, you have the needs of your constituents and your bureaucracy to satisfy. Do so and you get to stay; don't and you go away.

The whole vision thing starts with a clear definition of who is being served, and that definition must include each group that is important to success.

## 2. WHAT DO THOSE YOU SERVE VALUE THE MOST?

Remember the ego trap! What you think the customer needs is irrelevant; the only opinion that matters is the customer's. To build a strong vision you must listen to your customers carefully and continuously.

Sometimes customers will tell you about a problem, but won't be able to tell you about a solution.

> In the 1980s, busy phone customers said they needed to communicate more frequently from locations where there were no phones. One solution was to provide an increased number of conventional phones, so payphones popped up in public locations everywhere, and people started hanging out of car windows, dropping quarters, and making calls.
>
> The customers didn't say, "I want a cell phone," because they didn't know that was an option. But someone heard the customer talk about a need and envisioned something new. By linking the customer's need with new technology, something very valuable to the customer was created. It all started with someone listening carefully to a

*customer talk about a need and embracing change as a way to create value for the customers.*

Providing value always starts with listening to the customer.

## 3. HOW WILL YOU PROVIDE VALUE IN A DIFFERENTIATED WAY?

This is the toughest question. Every smart person you compete against is also trying to answer it.

The best way to win is by staying locked into meeting your customers' needs better than anyone else. Happily, this is also a satisfying way to spend your time. It feels good when those you serve say, "Thank you," because you have solved a problem or met a need. If you can keep yourself and your team focused on the good feelings associated with doing that, and keep politics and other unproductive activities minimized, you will have gone a long way toward differentiating your product or service.

In addition to this simple focus, the remainder of differentiation lies in doing the whole Checklist well. If you or your team's *commitment* level is higher than others, you will overcome more obstacles to meeting customers' needs than others will. If your *vision* is clearer and more complete, you will stay focused better. If your team has *better people, leadership, and balance* than others, it will outperform them. Combining good feelings from meeting customers' needs with strength in the other elements of The Checklist is the whole recipe for differentiation. You will be hard to beat with this package.

But remember: Circumstances are changing at an accelerating rate, so the specifics of how you create and sustain a competitive advantage must change also. Whether it's lower costs from foreign sourcing, a technology advantage, or a distribution advantage, it is sustainable only through continuous smart responses to changing customer needs linked to changing circumstances.

For example, if you rely on your selling expertise, a distribution channel shift can hurt you.

*Damark Corporation was a rapidly growing, publicly traded company that sold merchandise through catalogs…until Internet sales provided the same products to consumers faster and cheaper. The availability of this new, fast, low-cost distribution channel to consumers killed the business.*

In our shrinking world, all manufacturers must consider buying from non-U.S. sources or risk becoming cost uncompetitive.

*Wal-Mart was once known as the company that bought all its merchandise in America. I recently checked ten items on a Wal-Mart shelf, and none was made in the U.S.A.*

Vision revision means success; vision paralysis means failure.

Differentiation starts with listening to customers' needs and then focusing on deriving satisfaction from meeting those needs. If your process of listening and revisioning works well and never ends, you can succeed long term. If your revisioning process fails to work well or ends, so will your team.

## 4. HOW WILL YOU SUSTAIN THE EFFORT FINANCIALLY?

The answer to this question is that you must remain sharply focused so that everything you do directly relates to providing maximum value to your customers. There are two basic parts to remaining focused:

+ *Margin Generation.* Margin is the difference between what customers pay you and what it costs you to provide the product or service. Successful visions focus on both increasing the highest margin activities and reducing lower margin activities. If you are a non-profit, charity, educator, or bureaucrat, you may substitute some other measure for margin (such as the number of needy persons served or number of students with high test scores). The point here is to increase focus on whatever generates the most value and decrease focus on whatever generates the least value. It seems obvious, but an amazing number of people feed activities with low margins and starve activities with high margins. Don't do it. Focus on your winning activities.

+ *Cost Control*. Anything that provides great value to your customers is really important (remember the ego trap—your opinion is irrelevant and only the customer's opinion counts). If you spend a dollar and it directly provides value to those you serve, it's an important dollar. If the dollar does not directly provide value, it's a less important dollar. Revise spending to focus on what's most important to your customers. This sounds simplistic, but it's surprising how much money is spent on stuff that customers don't care about. Spend money only on what smart customers care about.

A simple way to implement this thinking is to ask spending questions from your best customers' perspectives.

Would your best customers want you to buy this piece of equipment, implement this system, or hire this person? Would your best customer see the expenditure for a new building as providing added value or just adding to cost? Using this perspective helps you make wise spending decisions.

Focus on putting more of the highest margin work through your system, and focus on spending that provides direct value to your customers. Things can become more complicated if you add factors such as "We must grow by 15 percent per year" to the picture. Then you must spend wisely today on that which will generate the greatest value in the future. But, in the end, the strongest team will be the one that focuses on its highest margin opportunities and spends the least on things customers don't care about.

## SUMMARY: A LEADER'S MOST IMPORTANT TASK

If you are a leader, you have no more important job than creating and maintaining a winning vision. It's the foundation upon which everything is built. And today's vision and plans must evolve continuously, because they will be wrong in the near future as conditions change.

Whether you are the CEO, a department head, a supervisor, or a team leader, you are the person who defines the vision for your group. Right visions yield success; wrong visions yield failure. Stay focused on customers' needs—meeting those needs and making a profit. If you do, you can win. If you don't, someone who is better focused will beat you.

## PEARL #3

EVERY SALE STARTS
WITH LISTENING.

Remember the ego trap and get
yourself out of the way. Step one
in providing value to those you
serve is always the same—listen
carefully to determine what they
need. You can't listen if you're
talking.

## PEARL #4

IF IT'S A WINNER, PUMP IT.
IF IT'S A LOSER, DUMP IT.

Focus energy where the return
is greatest. Determine where the
best and worst margins are and
then proactively move toward the
best margins.

## PEARL #5

YOUR PLAN WILL BE
WRONG TOMORROW.

Something will change soon.
The change may relate to technology, foreign competition, new
materials, faster communication,
distribution channel shifts, new
systems, changing competitor
strategies, etc. The only thing you
can count on is that something is
changing, and your plan will soon
need revision in response to the
change.

## WHAT'S NEXT?

When the vision is strong, it is people who kill it or bring it to life.

# CHAPTER FIVE

# People

## CHECKPOINT #3: "Is the Team a Clear Winner?"

Nothing is more important than the performance of people, and nothing is more painful than the failure of people to perform. Assessing people's performance and solving people problems can remain complex and painful, or it can become simpler and less painful through using the concepts in this chapter.

## WINNING TEAMS

Everything that gives you a competitive advantage—new services, products, concepts, and systems—originates in someone's mind. If that person is on your team, you win. If they aren't, you lose.

The only way to build a sustainable advantage is to have the best people, retain them, and focus them on providing value to your customers at a profit (remember that profit will be defined in terms other than dollars if you are not dealing with a business issue). Other than having a right vision, nothing is more important to success than gathering and retaining people who provide winning performances.

Good people are your greatest assets, while dysfunctional people are the greatest threat to success.

> *We the people of the United States, in oxdex to foxm a moxe pexfect union, establish justice, insuxe domestic txanquility, pxovide fox the common defense, pxomote the genexal welfaxe and secuxe the blessing of libexty to ouxselves and oux Postexity, do oxdain and establish this Constitution fox the United States of Amexica.*

This beautiful and powerful statement has been ruined because of one dysfunctional element. If the "r" represents a dysfunctional person on your team, you can see the damage being done. No matter how committed you are, how good your vision is, and how effective the other people are, the whole thing becomes a mess when one element, one person, is dysfunctional.

## DYSFUNCTIONAL PEOPLE

Few tasks are more painful than dealing with people problems. They're so painful we often avoid dealing with them until we are backed into a corner and forced to take action.

Why are these problems so painful? One major reason is because we focus on the wrong issues. We ask questions such as "Is this a good person?" "Is this person trying to do a good job?" and "Am I being too hard on this person?" These are tough questions because they are very subjective, and we are reluctant to impose our value systems on others when the person's job is at risk. But *these are the wrong questions, and asking them makes your task more difficult.* There is a clearer, less painful way to determine if a person is dysfunctional in their job.

## DYSFUNCTIONAL PERSON TEST

Here's how to make it easier: The three things your team must have to be successful are satisfied customers, productive teammates, and profit. If a person is contributing to these three, the person is effective. If a person is continually damaging any of these, the person is dysfunctional. The Dysfunctional Person Test involves just three questions:

**1** Is this person hurting customer satisfaction?

Yes _____ No _____

**2** Is this person hurting good teammates? Yes _____ No _____

**3** Is this person hurting profits?    Yes _____ No _____

After walking into failing companies with dysfunctional

people for over thirty years, I know the Dysfunctional Person Test is right. If you consider a certain person and answer "Yes" to any of these questions, the person is dysfunctional and there is a problem. If you get more than one "Yes," the person is a big problem. And if the person is a senior person, you have an enormous problem, because everyone subordinate to that person is being hurt, and good people will leave rather than tolerate the dysfunctional person.

## TWO TYPICAL CHARACTERISTICS OF DYSFUNCTIONAL PEOPLE

*1. Look for the Takers in Your Organization.*

To identify dysfunctional people, distinguish between the Givers and Takers. Givers brighten your day. You trust them. When they are around, time flies, you feel energized, and things get done. It's like 1 + 1 = 3.

> *I was young, inexperienced, and managing a turnaround with operations from California to New Jersey. Dan reported to me and ran our Texas operations. We bounced ideas off each other. Sometimes we agreed, and sometimes we disagreed, but he always did the same thing. He took positive action by listening to me, applying his experience to the issues, implementing what we agreed on,*

*and improving his organization's performance. He let me*
*know what he was doing and did his job without fanfare.*
*We got a lot done…fast. Dan was a Giver.*

Takers are the people you worry about. You check on them frequently. When you're with a Taker, time slows down, it's no fun, and you feel tired. It's like 1 + 1 = 1.

*In this same turnaround, Tom ran the Midwest opera-*
*tions. He and I also talked frequently. Sometimes we*
*agreed, and sometimes we disagreed, but he seemed to put*
*spin on information he gave me and didn't implement the*
*ideas we agreed on, so I couldn't trust him. We began dis-*
*agreeing more often, and his operation made no improve-*
*ments. I worried every day about the impact he was hav-*
*ing as he consolidated power in his office and became a*
*tyrant with his people.*

In Tom's case, I resisted making a decision until the pain was just too great. As soon as I applied the Dysfunctional Person Test, it became crystal clear that Tom was performing badly. His customers weren't happy, his people weren't happy, and his decisions were hurting profitability. It was a no-brainer—Tom was dysfunctional, and we had to take immediate action, especially because he was in a senior position and was causing pain in all his good subordinates.

Don't confuse a Taker with someone who disagrees with you. Tom was dysfunctional because he failed the three-question test, not because he disagreed with me. If motivations are right, disagreement is good. Dan and Tom both disagreed with me. The difference was their motivations. Dan was concerned about the right things: Customer satisfaction, employee morale, and profits. Tom was concerned about selfish things designed to get him power and increased control over others. When Dan and I disagreed, it was about how to improve things for the benefit of all. When Tom and I disagreed, it was linked to Tom's ego needs. Disagreements with Tom made me tired, but I welcomed the disagreements with Dan because we improved things. Disagreements driven by the right motivations are good; disagreements driven by selfish or ego-based motivations are bad.

2. *Continuous Damage Control.*
The second way to identify dysfunctional people is to look where you do continuous damage control. Are any of your good team members constantly fixing problems that start in another person's area of responsibility? If so, then look where the problems originate and you will probably find a dysfunctional person—someone who is creating problems

rather than solving them. That person's failure to perform is hurting the team because other good people are doing their job plus cleaning up behind the dysfunctional person. Take corrective action immediately.

> *The salesman was a wonderful guy and very likable, but that wasn't the issue. His jobs always seemed to have problems. Our production people were constantly cleaning up errors and omissions in his documentation. Our accounting people frequently had to make adjustments and give credits to his customers because of misunderstandings. The result was constant internal frustration and, when the production and accounting people couldn't get the problems solved fast enough, customers were dissatisfied.*
>
> *The cause of the problem was not in accounting or production, though that is where our people spent so much time fixing the problems. It was in the salesman because he failed to solve problems at the front end of jobs. Our customers were dissatisfied, and good employees were frustrated. The salesman was dysfunctional, and his failure to perform needed fixing.*

When I applied the Dysfunctional Person Test to this salesman, the answer was obvious. Despite the fact that he was a great guy, he was creating unhappy customers, causing frustration in other employees, and hurting profits. He was clearly dysfunctional.

## FOUR STEPS TO BUILDING A STRONG TEAM
### 1. Eliminate Dysfunctional People.

It starts with the three-question Dysfunctional Person Test. Being a dysfunctional person is not about being a good or bad person. If someone is repeatedly hurting customer satisfaction, reducing the effectiveness of other good team members, or damaging profits, they do not fit your team and can't stay in the job. This standard is pragmatic, not moralistic, and removes the painful uncertainty linked to moralistic judgments.

> *Sharon was at the receptionist desk every day and did her record-keeping tasks well. But customers commented that she seemed irritated with them and was a little abrupt. She was hurting customer satisfaction. After some discussion, Sharon admitted she really didn't like interacting with the customers and preferred to work by herself. She was transferred into data entry and has been happy ever since. She was dysfunctional in a customer contact role but excellent in data entry.*

## 2. Gather the Best.

Protect your best performers and replace your poorest performers. The team with the best roster from top to bottom will usually win.

*After months of trying to improve Tom's operations, we had to replace him. Bob and Jim worked for a competitor and were in charge of Production and Sales respectively. Their company had new ownership, and we heard that these two men were unhappy. After a series of meetings, it became clear that Bob and Jim understood about meeting customers' needs, had high regard for their subordinates, and knew how to make a profit. We hired them. In the next several months they improved customer satisfaction, morale skyrocketed, and profits grew steadily. Meanwhile, after they departed, the competitor struggled and eventually closed. Replacing Tom with Bob and Jim made all the difference.*

> "EAGLES DON'T FLOCK—
> YOU HAVE TO FIND
> THEM ONE AT A TIME."
> —Ross Perot

Every team has a normal range of performers with a few top performers, many mid-range performers, and a few poor performers. This is true at each level in your organization—from the most senior people to the most junior people. A winning strategy requires that you not only immediately replace dysfunctional people, but also continually replace poor performers with better performers at each level. These two actions raise the average performance level of your team. If you do this more effectively than your competitors, you will have a better roster and a competitive advantage. If you don't, you'll be at a competitive disadvantage and failure is more likely.

### 3. Set Clear Expectations.

The expectations you communicate must be the same as those by which you measure performance. Don't preach one

**"NOBODY RISES TO LOW EXPECTATIONS."**
—Calvin Lloyd

set of expectations to your team and measure performance based on something else. Many otherwise skillful leaders can get caught in this trap.

At one time I was guilty of saying that my expectations were defined in our EAT program (Excellence, Attitude, and Teamwork), while in reality I used the Dysfunctional Person Test to measure performance. The team was busy focusing on Excellence through continuous improvement, positive Attitudes toward all persons and events, and Teamwork to get things done well together. Meanwhile, I was measuring people's performance based on their achievement of customer satisfaction, their impact on other employees, and their contribution to profit. Both they and I were confused until I replaced the EAT concept expectations with the standards I was really using.

The three questions in the Dysfunctional Person Test provide a clear and simple set of expectations. You expect your team members to contribute to high levels of:

- Customer satisfaction.
- Teammate effectiveness and morale.
- Profit.

Complicated expectations are nearly useless. Make them simple and useful. Simple is better.

> I visited a friend's company. On the shop floor I casually asked a woman how she was doing that day. Her answer was wonderful. She said, "I made the 50 units we needed today, and all of them passed inspection. And I gave the supervisor a suggestion."
>
> In that simple summary she hit the three critical points. Customer satisfaction was accomplished by producing the number of units that were needed. She helped a fellow employee, her supervisor, by offering a suggestion. And she contributed to profit by getting her work done with no defective units. I suspect she went home feeling good that day because she knew what was expected and she did it.

Do yourself and everyone around you a favor and be clear

about what you expect. I suggest that you clearly state your expectations in terms of customer satisfaction, helping teammates, and generating profit so your people are not surprised when you measure performance that way.

## HOW DO YOU KEEP EXPECTATIONS FOCUSED?

Question: What's the biggest problem with performance evaluations? Answer: They don't get done. Question: Why don't they get done? Answer: People generally avoid confrontation/conflict and feel that the time, energy, and pain involved with doing the evaluations isn't worth the benefit derived from them. Result: People avoid doing evaluations or delay them as much as possible.

> *Scenario 1. In this large company the employee review forms required the manager to analyze many topics and write narratives on various issues. The process required hours of preparation by the supervisor because the forms were comprehensive. The process was so demanding that the supervisor had delayed doing them this time and skipped them previously. When she finally completed the forms and the employee review meeting, she wasn't certain that the one really important problem had received adequate attention. She said to herself, "Maybe it's just not worth all the effort."*

*Scenario 2. In this small company there were no employee review forms and no formal employee review meetings. But good employees wanted feedback so they knew where they stood, could fix problems their managers were concerned about, and could improve in areas that would help them get promoted. When review meetings happened, the employee usually forced the situation by asking for a meeting, and the supervisor had to take time to figure out how to make the meeting productive. The meetings didn't happen very often and were painful.*

If people are your most valuable asset, isn't it important to keep them focused and correct dysfunctional behaviors? Obviously it is. So what can you do about the problem? Answer: Use Stop/Start/Continue (SSC).

SSC is an effective way to do employee reviews. It uses a simple form, concentrates on the most important issues, and works from both sides of the senior/subordinate relationship, providing constructive feedback to both parties. Here's how it works:

1. Prior to the meeting, both the senior and the subordinate get a page with three sections: Stop, Start, and Continue. The senior writes down the most important things the subordinate should stop doing, start

doing, and continue doing. There may or may not be action items for all three sections. The subordinate does the same for the senior, writing things that the supervisor should stop, start, and continue doing.

2. At the review meeting, one or the other volunteers to go first and starts with the items in the Stop section. Those items get discussed until they are understood. Then the other person explains their Stop items, and they get discussed.

3. The process continues through Start and Continue.

4. At the end of the meeting, both parties know what is most important to the other and the issues have been discussed.

The process has fairness and balance that produces mutual respect and well-intentioned thoughts. Both the senior and subordinate have said what is important to them, and extraneous topics haven't clouded the key issues. Both people are invested in the process, and both people feel good because their thoughts have been honored. Good things happen.

> *Paul was a project manager who reported to me. We had worked together for about six months, and he was doing some things that bothered me. It was time for a Stop/Start/ Continue.*

Paul had never been through an SSC before and didn't know what to expect. After I gave him the simple form and told him how the process worked, we each jotted down our thoughts as they occurred to us over the next week.

Our meeting dealt with no extraneous issues; it focused only on what was most important to the two of us. I explained to Paul that he was doing a fine job in most ways, but I wanted him to stop being confrontational with the production people, because that was producing conflict between him and the shop. He said he wanted me to start supporting his projects better, so he could get them done on time. We started our discussion with very different perspectives on the two issues, but after some time we saw each other's perspectives much more clearly. Paul began to realize that operations had to balance production time among several key customers, only one of which was Paul's, and I realized that Paul never actually saw me do things that helped his projects, so he was unaware of what I was doing to support him.

With a new, clearer understanding of each other's perspectives, we built a foundation for trust and worked well together thereafter. Compared to fixing these two issues, nothing else was very important to us, and we both felt good about getting the problems resolved. We spent a little time on SSC and got a solid return on that time *investment. Since then one or the other of us has called for an SSC meeting on a couple occasions when an important topic needed discussion.*

SSC is simple and effective. Why do something more complicated that is less effective?

### Focused Incentive Plans

There are always many things that need to get done, but sometimes there is one action that stands alone in importance. It's the thing that, all by itself, can make the difference between success and failure. For instance, if the nonprofit doesn't increase donations by 30 percent, it will be forced to close. Or if the shop doesn't improve productivity by 10 percent, the company will lose money. Or if the team doesn't reduce the opponents' shots-on-goal by 25 percent, it is likely to lose.

In scenarios such as these, if the group performs normally in all other aspects and also accomplishes these particular actions, it can succeed—if not, it fails. Accomplishing these specific actions is critical. What's the best way to get them done?

Focused incentive plans are a powerful tool to help you complete these actions. But many incentive programs fail because of two common mistakes:

- The program is too complicated for the participants to understand.
- The program rewards actions the participants don't directly control so they can't produce results.

*The company was losing money and needed to decrease costs. The new bonus program in the distribution center was intended to reward improved performance. Expected cost savings would fund the cost of the incentive payments with money left over to improve earnings.*

*The program designers decided to pay incentives for four important activities: On-time shipments, complete shipments, reduced damage to merchandise, and timely processing of return items. Measurements were created for each task. Progress was tracked by summing the performance increases and decreases in each of the four activities. But the calculations were so complicated that the employees didn't understand them and participants watched the numbers go up and down with no apparent correlation to what they did individually. It was confusing.*

*In the end, the employees did their individual jobs as best they could, but no one understood how they could really make a difference. No one really felt as though they had much impact. Minor progress was made and small bonuses were paid, but everyone agreed the program needed to be overhauled or scrapped.*

Conversely, powerful results come from focused incentive programs.

*When I took over the company, it was generating big losses and was on the verge of bankruptcy, so we had to improve cash flow quickly. We had to increase our gross margin dollars, and we had three ways to do it: Increase the number of sales leads, increase our closing percentage, and increase the gross margin dollars we received on each sale. I created this simple financial model: Gross margin $ = Number of leads x Closing percentage x Gross margin per sale.*

*After going on several sales calls, I realized we were priced under the competition, so step one was to raise prices. That would increase our gross margin $ per sale, while we maintained our closing percentages. We raised prices and paid bonuses to every sales person who maintained their historic closing percentage. It worked. The price increases took effect, and the salespeople maintained their closing percentages to earn the bonuses.*

*We achieved positive cash flow quickly.*

*Once our people knew they could sell at higher prices, we emphasized the second critical action—improving closing percentages. We offered a proven sales training program, but the people had to pay a portion of the cost up front and we would repay them this amount if they satisfactorily completed the course. This made each person commit to completing the training. Once they realized how much more commission they could earn from a 10 percent closing percentage increase compared to the modest cost of the training, they all signed up for it. It worked.*

*At the end of the second year we had both higher prices and higher closing percentages.*

*In the third year we focused on the third priority— lead generation. Our advertising cost per lead was high, but referral leads generated by salespeople were free, so we offered bonuses to salespeople who generated referral leads. The result was increased referral leads.*

*At the end of the three-phase program we had achieved substantial improvement in each of the three critical activities and the business was strong. Each of these programs required energy and focus. By doing one at a time our people focused on the most critical task and reaped the reward.*

Focused incentive plans will get the most critical task accomplished when the plan is simple enough for the participants to understand it and the participants have direct control over the action that must be accomplished.

Resist the temptation to do too much at once! If you're aggressive, you'll want to do too many tasks at once and will fail to get the results you want as in Scenario 1 above. Don't do it! Create a simple program focused on actions the participants directly control.

## 4. TERMINATE PEOPLE RIGHT.

Despite your best efforts to gather the best people, set clear expectations, and keep people focused, you'll have team members who are poor performers. If you're unclear about what to do, use the Dysfunctional Person Test. If any answers are "Yes," take action now to end the pain and the damage.

> *During the past thirty years I've terminated hundreds of people, but this was the most painful termination of my career. Pat was the manager of a group that reported to me. For six months I thought I was sending clear signals that he wasn't meeting my expectations. We had many meetings about the issues, and I told him I was expecting improvement, but he wasn't receiving what I thought I was transmitting. On the day I terminated him, he broke down and cried, saying he never saw it coming. I had failed to communicate clearly enough and vowed never to make that mistake again.*

To terminate right, do the following:

First, meet with the person and tell them in the

plainest, most direct language possible where they fall short on the three questions. If their job is at risk, they deserve clear understanding of what's expected. Make them repeat the expectations and have them explain how they are falling short. If there is some circumstance or problem that is genuinely hurting their performance, and it is under your control and is correctable (for instance, getting them information they don't currently have or fixing some other manageable problem), then fix the problem immediately.

Second, give the person a short period of time (days not weeks) to change and meet expectations. If they do, recognize it and reinforce the improved behavior. If they don't, meet again *soon* and do plain talk again backed up by a written explanation. Many people will resign at this point rather than be fired, if they can't meet expectations.

Third, if they still fail to meet expectations after another short period, move them out of the job quickly. In a larger company you may be able to place them in other suitable work rather than terminate them. That's less likely in a smaller company.

Fourth, if termination is necessary, a short meeting is less painful for everyone than a long one. Keep the discussion focused only on facts from previous meetings and don't introduce new issues. Details of termination arrangements should be thought through in advance and presented in writing so there is no confusion or need for follow-up meetings. Get the pain over quickly so everyone can move on.

## SUMMARY

Individuals who perform well together are what bring the vision to life. Continuously improve your team. Dysfunctional individuals nullify all the good things done by other team members. Minimize the difficulty of identifying dysfunctional people by using the Dysfunctional Person Test. Be totally honest and direct as you discuss expectations and problems with the person. If the person remains dysfunctional, remove him or her quickly. Other than being adequately committed and having a winning vision, nothing is more critical to success than doing this well.

## PEARL #6

HIRE SLOW AND FIRE FAST.

This sounds brutal, but it's pragmatic. Bring people into your team as carefully as possible, because the consequences of adding a dysfunctional person are pain and trouble. And when you know someone is dysfunctional, take action quickly to minimize the damage.

## WHAT'S NEXT?

No matter how good your team is, sooner or later you'll face serious problems that you didn't expect. In these situations strong crisis leadership is essential to survival.

# CHAPTER SIX

# Leadership

## CHECKPOINT #4:
### "Will the Leaders Handle Crises Well?"

Crises cause natural selection in organizations. Winners are separated from losers very quickly because winners survive and losers don't. The difference between the two lies in the effectiveness of the crisis leader.

In simple terms, there are two leadership environments—good times and bad times. We'll summarize leadership in good times quickly and then focus on the critical topic of leadership in crises.

## LEADERSHIP IN GOOD TIMES

In good times the leader must accomplish many things, including but not limited to:

- Create and communicate a winning vision.
- Revise the vision in response to changing conditions.
- Create organizational structures that serve the vision.
- Create systems that support the vision.
- Recruit, motivate, focus, and retain the best people.
- Define expectations and establish a culture that nurtures those expectations.
- Do all the above in a way that is sustainable.

Because a rising tide floats all ships, many leadership styles can succeed in good times. Observers may have difficulty determining whether the leader is highly skilled or poorly skilled because things will generally be getting better. And when times are good, we tend to enjoy prosperity and be less critical.

All this is not to say that leadership is easy in good times. There are perpetual challenges that require strong commitment, disciplined revisioning, continual assessment of people-performance issues, and a broad range of other skills. But more people can manage in good times when survival issues are not immediate than can manage in crises when the consequences of failure are immediate and cruel.

## LEADERSHIP IN CRISES

No matter how good your vision is and how capable your people are, unexpected crises will happen.

*A close friend skillfully led his public company through twenty-six consecutive quarters of record sales and profits. By any standard his performance was exceptionally good, and he was recognized by all as an excellent leader. Then, unexpectedly, international events over which he had no control caused his major markets to evaporate, creating chaos in his industry. The company's stock plummeted, and he was held accountable. I'll never forget him saying, "I wasn't as good as they said I was on the way up…and wasn't as bad as they said I was on the way down."*

*This man had been a high achiever his entire life. He was a team-leading athlete and had graduated at the top of his class at business school and law school. He worked diligently in the same business for over twenty years, serving in a variety of capacities. Yet despite all that preparation, knowledge, and commitment, circumstances combined that caused havoc in his business.*

*He was neither a superstar nor a loser? He was a good person that worked hard and got caught in circumstances that created a crisis.*

Sooner or later circumstances beyond your control will create a mess. Your team will be forced to react and will win or lose according the rules of your game. During the crisis, your team will either feel good or bad about their performance. If they feel good, confidence grows and the team becomes stronger. If they feel bad, confidence decreases, making the team weaker. The bigger the crisis, the bigger the effect. So handling big crises well is a critical part of long-term success.

> In the 1980s, Chrysler Corporation was in a mess and the media declared it was headed for bankruptcy. Observers described the company as debt ridden and internally dysfunctional. Its various brands had been losing market share to competitors for many years.
>
> Just prior to WWII, England's navy was decrepit and was being decimated by German submarines. British air forces had good planes but were short on skilled pilots, and her land forces were poorly equipped and unprepared for war as the nation faced a Nazi juggernaut poised for invasion.
>
> Both of these crises could have been catastrophic, but Chrysler and England emerged successfully and with renewed strength. What did they have in common? In both scenarios a leader emerged who guided them through the crisis to success.

**THE SPEED OF THE BOSS IS THE SPEED OF THE TEAM.** —Lee Iacocca

In bad times, successful crisis leaders must do four things well or the situation will get worse fast. They must:

*1. Become Highly Visible and Very Active.*
Iacocca and Churchill did not hide in their offices. Both continually rallied their people through speeches and appearances.

*2. Define the Problem Clearly and Create a Vision*
*for Action to Which People Can Attach Emotionally.*
Both Iacocca and Churchill defined the challenge as life or death. Churchill's "We will meet them on the beaches…" speech created a vision of defiant heroism that made every Briton a warrior. Iaccoca preached customer focus as the path to survival until every Chrysler person wanted it.

*3. Emit Energy That Sparks Exceptional Performance.*
Both Iacocca and Churchill worked energetically and in doing so they set a standard that inspired those around them.

*4. Follow Through on the Plan Until the Crisis Is Past.*
Beyond the appearances and speeches, both Iacocca and Churchill worked skillfully behind the scenes. Iaccoca led new product development teams, dealer focus groups, refinancing efforts, and advertising campaigns. Churchill negotiated Lend-Lease with the U.S. to acquire weaponry and finance a military buildup as he also solidified other alliances and executed his internal defense plan.

Churchill and Iaccoca were crisis leader role models, but on a smaller scale everyday heroes also lead their groups through trouble. Admiral "Bull" Halsey led U.S. naval forces in the Pacific after the Japanese attacked Pearl Harbor at the beginning of World War II. As Americans fought for survival, he saw many acts of heroism and concluded that heroes were ordinary people who were thrust into extraordinary circumstances and did what they felt they had to do.

## EVERYDAY HEROES

*Lavonne was a petite blonde in Florida redneck country, and the place she worked at was in trouble. She spoke up when things weren't right and followed her words with long hours of hard work. Her energy, sincerity, and dedication inspired higher levels of productivity and quality among the other employees as she advanced from her job as a worker on the third shift to the Assistant Plant Manager job. The improvements she generated saved the plant from being shut down.*

*Steve was the number two executive in a Fortune 500 company, but he wanted to do something that felt more important. He left his lofty position to found and lead a non-profit company focused on getting indigent minority men into good jobs by helping them improve their self-con-*

cept. No one had figured out how to do this consistently, but he worked tirelessly for several years through repeated defeats until he created a program that worked. His vision and steadfast commitment have improved the lives of many forgotten people.

Terri was a farmer's wife whose smile and energy were infectious. As the Customer Service Supervisor in a struggling company, she assumed responsibility for solving tough problems. She was at work every day and took on one difficult situation after another. Her commitment to getting things done and doing the right thing formed a core around which the troubled business built its service ethic, enabling survival of the company.

O.H. was short and built like a fireplug. He was an old-style, hardworking, commonsense production manager who willingly stepped into a plant that had a labor relations mess. By rolling up his sleeves and digging into the day-to-day details of the operation, he gained the trust of his men. It took a year, but at the end of that effort he had defused his 80 militant New Jersey union guys. He saved their jobs by focusing them on getting the work done rather than fighting with management.

Each of these folks did the four key things that effective crisis leaders do. They assumed a visible, and therefore risky, position; defined the challenge in a way people could attach to emotionally; sparked excellent performance in others because of the high standards they set; and followed through every day until the crisis was over. They weren't born heroes. They were normal people who faced trouble and did what effective crisis leaders do.

As you assess your challenge, ask yourself who'll step into the leadership role when trouble comes. If the person is you, ask yourself if you want to do it and if you're up to the task. If it's not you, who will take charge? Do you completely trust that person to do a great job?

Your answer is critical because sooner or later trouble will come, and after the trouble your team will be weaker or stronger based on how the leader performs. If the problem is big and an effective leader emerges, you'll succeed and be stronger. If no effective leader emerges, your team may die.

## CHARACTERISTICS OF EFFECTIVE CRISIS LEADERS

Effective crisis leaders tend to have some common traits. Ask yourself if you or others will be an effective crisis leader and use these traits as indicators:

*1. Clear Understanding of the Vision.*
Effective crisis leaders keep their team focused on achieving

the vision—who are your customers, what do they value most, how do you provide differentiated value, and how do you make a profit—rather than on the threat. Winning in a crisis means accomplishing the vision despite the distractions of the crisis. It requires simultaneous defense against external attacks and aggressive internal actions to build strength quickly.

> *Even though Chrysler was fighting financial battles and getting beaten up in the media, Iaccoca had to focus his team on giving customers what they wanted or there'd be no money or time to do anything else. Even though Churchill had to deal with continuous air and submarine attacks and espionage threats, he had to negotiate Lend-Lease, solidify external alliances, and build internal infrastructure for his nation's defense.*

*2. No One Can Do Everything Well. Plug the Holes.*
To get out of a crisis, many things must be done fast and well. But none of us are perfect; we're not proficient at everything. Effective leaders focus on using their personal strengths well and then fill in their weaknesses, trusting capable people to plug the holes.

> *Think of a beautiful scene pictured in a jigsaw puzzle. To create it you assemble pieces that have parts that stick out*

*(strengths) and parts that recede (weaknesses). When you
put all the pieces together, you create the beautiful picture.
But if you leave any pieces out, you create holes and the picture is ruined.*

*It's like that with teams. Each player has strengths
and weaknesses, including the leader. The effective crisis
leader plays to his strengths and covers his weaknesses.
He assembles players who complement one another, cover
all the critical tasks, and get the job done well. If the team
is assembled quickly, the effort can proceed rapidly. If the
leader's ego gets in the way or the leader fails to recognize
weaknesses that need to be filled, your team can fail.*

### 3. Trustworthiness Is a Big Deal.

Does the team trust the leader? The more serious the
situation, the more trust is required. When a group feels
a serious threat, they want strong leadership because
good people may quit rather than follow someone they
don't trust. Conversely, many people will go through hell
with someone they trust completely.

*Ghandi was an extraordinarily effective crisis leader
because of his trustworthiness. People knew he was willing to starve himself to death for their cause, so they followed him through very difficult times.*

## 4. Walk the Talk.

"Your actions speak so loudly I can't hear your words." I don't know who first said this, but I know it's true.

> *Firefighters follow the first person into a burning building. Alcoholics Anonymous attendees share after the first person tells their story. The first donors get charitable giving started.*

People who talk a good show but cower before adversity are dangerous, because they won't perform when you need them to lead. If you have a proven crisis leader, your team has an important resource. If you have no proven crisis leader, your team is vulnerable unless one emerges. This checkpoint may not seem critical right now (unless you're in a crisis), but sooner or later events will unfold that demand a crisis leader, and the survival of your team depends on that person's performance.

> "SUCCESSFUL LEADERS HAVE THE COURAGE TO TAKE ACTION WHILE OTHERS HESITATE."
> —John Maxwell

## SUMMARY

Crisis leaders aren't hardwired for greatness at birth. They are normal people who choose to do the four things that crisis leaders do when they face trouble. Given that sooner or later a crisis will happen, your team will do well only if someone:

- Takes control visibly and immediately.
- Defines the challenge simply and creates a vision for action that people attach to emotionally.
- Emits energy that sparks exceptional performance.
- Follows through, completing critical tasks, until the problem is solved.

Effective crisis leaders understand these actions and execute them when crises arise. Bosses will be effective crisis leaders only if they understand these actions and execute them when times are tough. Some bosses use titles and trappings for power; leaders use strength of character and integrity. Crisis leaders can be bosses, but not all bosses can be crisis leaders. Recognize the difference between the two, because survival in a crisis depends on leaders not bosses.

## WHAT'S NEXT?

If you've passed the commitment, vision, people, and leadership checkpoints, there's just one more. It's very simple but immensely important.

# CHAPTER SEVEN

# Balance

## CHECKPOINT #5:
### "Will Loved Ones Get What They Need?"

In the end, nothing is more important than your loving relationships. You may own the world, but without love and loved ones you have nothing.

## FINDING BALANCE

Success is seductive. Recognition, money, power, travel, and creating things are great ego inflators. Are you being seduced? Are you addicted to success?

How many people do you know who've lost a relationship with their son, daughter, wife, husband, or other loved one because they focused on something that excluded that loved one? I know too many.

> "IT'S A GOOD THING TO BE RICH AND STRONG, BUT IT'S A BETTER THING TO BE LOVED."
> —Euripides

Have past achievements hurt your loving relationships?

Will your commitment to the current challenge hurt them?

If the answer is "Yes," then don't deceive yourself…you are losing, not winning.

*You've seen Hershel if you watched the original SEAL documentary on the Discovery Channel. He's the big guy with the shaved head, giant handlebar mustache, bushy eyebrows, and eyes that sparkle and pierce at the same time. Hershel stayed in the Teams as long as they would have him and achieved the very senior rank of Master Chief Petty Officer. He describes his experience as "Been there, done that, and got the T-shirt." Two stub-fingers on his left hand give evidence that he's been on the wrong end of a gun once too often.*

*What he did during his career was intoxicating, addictive, and seductive. The call of faraway places, doing secret things with men who were exceptionally skilled and totally committed made normal life seem boring and trivial. But when he left the Teams, he found himself alone. His wife and family were the same strangers to him that they had been while he was an active SEAL, but the Team portion of his life was gone.*

*We talk often. He misses his family and wishes he had realized what he was doing to those relationships before the damage was beyond repair.*

# BALANCE IS NOT AN EITHER-OR PROPOSITION

*Ann was bright and driven. She excelled in school and was a star in her job. As her professional stature grew, she saw herself as a role model for women who wanted to crash through glass ceilings. Success fed on success, and her life was full…almost.*

*She and her husband had been running so hard and doing so well that they hadn't taken time to think about children. They suddenly realized that the time was approaching when it would be difficult or risky for Ann to have a baby…or two.*

*She almost panicked when the facts really sunk in.*

A very successful friend, Jim Campbell, once commented that "True champions are those who win not once, but year after year." That winning must be balanced between the challenges you select and the people you love.

Some people think balance is an either-or proposition. They see the issue as committing either to a challenge (as in work or some quest) or to their loved ones. But to lead a fulfilling life, both aspects need to be satisfied. Sometimes the challenge needs to get special emphasis, and sometimes your loved

> "WHO, BEING LOVED, IS POOR?" —Oscar Wilde

ones need extra attention. To be a true champion you must blend your commitment to achievements with your personal commitments so you succeed in both areas long term. Amassing a long list of achievements at the expense of loving relationships is not a winning performance.

## SHOULD YOU CLIMB THE MOUNTAIN?

*As I looked at Beck Wethers' misshapen face and the stubs that were once a surgeon's fingers, I flashed back...*

*Six of us young hotshots went to Russia in 1990 to climb the highest mountain in Europe, Mt. Elbrus. The other five guys had climbing experience; I thought I'd test myself to see if I could do it at forty-something.*

*Twin-peaked Elbrus reaches nearly 20,000 feet into the Georgian sky and is a windswept sheet of ice broken by rock above 15,000 feet. When the weather clears, visibility extends for a hundred miles. In bad weather, you may not even see your buddy five feet away, and the mountain becomes a killer. In our case the weather was bad.*

*I developed food poisoning the day we started the climb and was bedridden for two days with vomiting and diarrhea. Weakened but still determined, I caught up with the group at 14,000 feet.*

The weather had been vicious for two days, and on the third morning we had to make a decision because our visas were expiring. Though the blizzard was still blowing, we had to either go for the summit in the terrible weather or go down the mountain. Three other groups in base camp decided to go down, and one of our guys joined them. Five of us decided to go for the summit.

Our experience that day rivaled anything I experienced in the SEALs. We spent fourteen hours with no food or water, climbing continuously in gusts up to sixty miles per hour and a windchill factor around –95°F. Sometimes visibility was less than six feet. At one point Sasha (one of the guides) and I were separated from the group in a total whiteout. Sasha grabbed my arm and said something told him we should stop and sit down. We hunkered down, and the snow piled up on us. Half an hour later, when the storm weakened slightly, we saw a crevasse six feet in front of us. Amazing!

At the summit, one member of our group collapsed and wanted to give up. We were faced with a life-and-death decision, because if we left him he would freeze soon, and if we helped him and slipped, we would slide down the ice until we hit a rock or fell into a crevasse. Only courage and teamwork got us all down alive.

Did we rise to a challenge or let too much testosterone cloud our judgment? What were our priorities?

Ten years later as I listened to Beck Wethers, it was clear that I could have looked like him or something worse could have happened. Wethers is widely known as the survivor in the 1997 Mount Everest expedition. He was left for dead—twice—on the mountain, losing most of his face, hands, and feet to frostbite. Now this previously famous surgeon and adventurer describes what he learned through that monumental experience: Earlier in his life he was busy achieving things as an athlete, physician, and adventurer. Now nothing is more valuable to him than his loving relationships. When he had been left for dead and was fighting to survive, it was visions of his loved ones and his burning desire to be with them again that kept him alive when everything else was gone. Nothing else mattered. It took this extreme experience for him to learn what is really important. He no longer takes time with his loved ones for granted. He sees it as precious and makes certain it remains a top priority.

If you are considering a challenge—whether in your personal life or career—that can jeopardize your relationship with loved ones, be honest with yourself and with them as you make your decision.

## CHECK YOUR BALANCE

*1. Evaluate Your Life.*

Take several deep, slow breaths to relax. Now close your eyes, relax, and ask yourself two questions:

Do I have any regrets about past balance?

Yes _____ No _____

Is my current balance right or wrong?

Right ____Wrong _____

Don't over-think this; accept the first response that pops into your mind. If you have no doubt that your balance is right, that's good. If you have doubts that your balance is right, that's a problem that needs attention.

*2. Ask Your Best Non-Business Friends.*

If you ask your closest non-business related friends about your balance between chasing achievements and giving your loved ones the time and attention they need, what do they say? If you get answers that express no concern about your balance, that's great. But if the answers skirt the issue or suggest there is a problem, then your balance is questionable.

*3. Ask Your Loved Ones to Assess Your Balance.*

The people you are concerned about know if you are in

balance or not. Ask them. If they say you are giving them the time and attention they need, that's good. If they hesitate or their answers are not as positive as you would like, that's bad. You just got straight information from those you are most concerned about. Take it seriously.

*4. Do the Right Thing.*
As you consider the challenge you are facing, be certain you feel good about how it affects the Balance in your life.

## PEARL #7

TRUE CHAMPIONS DON'T
WIN JUST ONCE; THEY WIN
YEAR AFTER YEAR.

Winning with your loved ones
and in your other achievements
requires blending and balancing
the two. It's not an either-or; it's
a blend. Great success in one
and failure in the other is not
a winning performance.

# CHAPTER EIGHT

# Real-World Examples

S ooner or later everyone gets confused and asks, "What should I do?" In your personal life, it can be caused by thoughts about changing your work, accepting a new challenge, or making a financial investment.

> *I woke up at 5:30 a.m. and couldn't go back to sleep. My mind was spinning. I didn't know what to do, but I knew I had to do something. "What should I do?"*

In your professional life, competitive pressures, people problems, financial setbacks, technology changes, or other matters can throw your team off track and cause confusion.

> *I got into the office, sat down, and looked at the report. "Oh no! This is bad. What should I do?"*

Whether the issues are personal or professional, the brain pain and tight stomach will happen as waves of uncertainty wash over you.

There are two deadly diseases that we all suffer from: "I didn't know" attacks us when we are taking on a new challenge and haven't learned all the necessary lessons yet. "I knew but I forgot" attacks us when we repeat mistakes we've made previously. The antidote for both of these is to go back to the basics. Use The Checklist to identify the most important issues that need attention. Once you know which issues are most critical, you can create an effective action plan.

In this chapter, you'll find several real-world examples of how The Checklist worked to produce success. I hope these help you apply it to your specific situation.

## IS THIS A GOOD OPPORTUNITY OR NOT?

You have an opportunity before you, but is it right for you? We all face decisions about whether to accept new responsibilities and jobs. Here are two examples of how The Checklist helped me in these situations.

### The Big Deal

We were chasing an acquisition that would double our size, making us the largest player in our industry. All the bigger-is-better arguments made this seem smart and attractive.

We could get the best people, the best raw material prices, the best financing packages, and so on. So we chased the opportunity aggressively. The Checklist items kept us on track as we worked our way through Vision, People, and Leadership.

After a long day during which the team had most of The Checklist issues figured out and resolved, I stopped and asked myself the last Checklist question: "Will loved ones get what they need?"

The answer struck me like a punch in the stomach. I had been so busy chasing the deal with visions of money and recognition that I hadn't considered the personal price. Getting this deal done successfully meant that I would have to be away from home extensively for a year. And since things are usually harder than expected, the time away from home and the emotional demands would both be greater than anticipated. I wasn't willing to shift the balance in my life that much for that long. The price was too high.

We walked away from the deal, and it was a wise decision.

*Doing the Right Thing*

The charity was a good one, but they were struggling. I was very busy when they asked me to join their board. I didn't know what to do, so I pulled out The Checklist and came to the following conclusions:

*Checkpoint #1: Commitment—Is my commitment strong enough?* I liked the people who were involved, and I knew that the organization did good work. That felt good. But what about the specific commitments to money, time, and emotional energy? I could afford to make the financial contribution associated with being a board member, but the time commitment was another matter. Because the organization was struggling, I couldn't be sure how much time it would take for me to do a good job. And I knew that getting involved meant catching up on program, personnel, marketing, and financial issues before working on solutions and future planning. I wasn't clear about how much time it would take, but usually challenges take more time than expected. My answer was "Maybe," and I would have to clarify it.

*Checkpoint #2: Vision—Is the vision a clear winner?* Because the organization was struggling, the answer was an obvious "No." The vision may have good elements, but the overall vision was flawed because sustainability was in jeopardy—cash flow was insufficient, key staff were demoralized, and service to clients was beginning to suffer. The vision was not a winner at this point.

*Checkpoint #3: People—Is the team a clear winner?* Many of the program staff were wonderful people who cared deeply about those whom they served, so programs were still meeting clients needs well, but the staff was spread too thin. The financial problems told me that the leadership team was not satisfying the Dysfunctional Person Test as regards sustainability (making a profit). Someone or several people were failing to do their job and solve this problem, so the team was not a winner at this time.

*Checkpoint #4: Leadership—Will the leaders handle a crisis well?* The organization was struggling and on the verge of a crisis. The leadership was not getting the problems solved themselves. Crisis leadership was deficient.

*Checkpoint #5: Balance—Will loved ones get what they need?* The more I thought about the situation, the more time commitment, emotional commitment, and potential financial commitment I saw. My life was already busy. Doing a good job as a board member for this organization was going to take significant time from other areas of my life.

After going through The Checklist quickly, it was apparent that vision, people, and leadership problems were present. Doing my job well as a board member would consume significant personal time and family time. My commitment to helping the organization was not strong enough to do that. I made a financial contribution, but did not accept the board position.

## BUSINESS CASH FLOW IS BAD

Sooner or later it happens to everyone in business. You realize that things are not going well, profits are declining, and cash flow has turned negative. You can contemplate the situation, hoping for a flash that gives you an answer about what to do. Sometimes that happens, and sometimes the flash is right on. The more experienced you are, the more likely this will happen because you may have been there before and solved similar problems. If you get a flash (some folks call this intuition) and you trust it, then proceed based on the flash.

If, however, you consider the situation and just get a worse headache and a tighter stomach, then pull out The Checklist. It will give you structure as you think through the problem, and, if you're honest, it will lead you to the critical issues that need attention. You may not like what you find. The fixes for the problems may be difficult and complex. But you have two options: Play ostrich and stay in trouble or attack the right problems and work out a solution.

*Stop the Cash Flow Bleeding*

We'd been on a roll for three years, doing two acquisitions and growing our business, so we had both record sales and profits each year. We thought we were king of the hill with numbers like those. Then came 9/11 and a downturn.

The financial statements told the truth. Our cash position had been deteriorating consistently for several months. In the first month, I told myself that it was just a normal up-and-down situation and there was nothing to worry about. In the second month, I took it more seriously, but decided it was not a problem yet. In the third month, I decided that we had to take action to reverse the trend.

As I sat with my head in my hands, thoughts flashed through my mind, but no simple solution jumped out at me. So I pulled out my trusty Checklist and decided to go through it quickly.

*Checkpoint #1: Commitment—Is my commitment strong enough?* First, I checked on my time commitment. The hours I devoted to work were acceptable. Then I checked on money—the financial rewards were where I needed them to be. Emotional energy commitment was next. I liked the business and was making a contribution that I felt good about. This job was a good one, and I wanted to keep it. Conclusion: No problem with commitment; move on to the next checkpoint.

*Checkpoint #2: Vision—Is our vision a clear winner?* I knew we were in an economic downturn and had hoped that if we did our jobs well we could get through it without any pain. But the pain was here, so I better look hard at the vision thing.

First, "Who are our customers?" We had two divisions—commercial and residential. Commercial sales were two-thirds of our volume, but those customers were really feeling the downturn, and their purchases were clearly shrinking. The changing condition of our commercial customers and related shrinking sales was real and had to be factored into my action plan.

On the residential side, there was no decrease in market activity. It seemed that, despite the economic downturn, mortgage interest rates were so low that people were buying new homes and doing remodeling just like they had done before. Our residential sales volume and margins remained stable, and I knew there was business that we were not chasing. Why hadn't I seen that we needed to focus on growing this part of our business more aggressively?

Second, "What do our customers value most?" Our commercial customers still expected us to provide high quality products and on-time delivery, but now they watched their spending so closely that price was critical. In the past, our quality and service often got us orders even when our price was modestly higher, but recently I couldn't remember an order where our price was higher than a competitor's. Our commercial customers' increased demand for lower prices had to be addressed in my plan.

Residential customers' needs had continued stable. They wanted a good price, but they recognized that our quality and service was better than our competitors and they valued that so there wasn't any significant price pressure. That was good.

Third, "How do we differentiate ourselves so customers buy from us?" In commercial, it was clear that we had to reduce prices but maintain quality and service if we were going to get a bigger share of the pie. I needed to figure out how to reduce costs in my action plan.

In residential, our customers were satisfied because our sales volume was stable, and we actually had inquiries from potential customers we were not serving. I saw no need to change price, quality, service, or delivery.

Fourth, "How do we sustain our business?" This was a critical issue because cash flow was deteriorating. The commercial business rules had changed, and we either had to figure out how to lower costs so we could lower prices or accept lower sales volume and lower margins. Because commercial sales were so important to the business, a plan to maintain commercial volume and minimize margin reductions was a key action item.

The residential business was contributing good margins on sales. It was clear we needed a plan to increase these sales.

*Checkpoint #3: People—Is the team a clear winner?* On the commercial side, we had a key account salesman who had been with the company for over twenty years and was a fine person. But he was so nice that he couldn't give anyone bad news. So when he put orders into production, he sometimes didn't explain about the short lead time that would make on-time delivery nearly impossible. And then when our operations people couldn't get the products delivered to the customer on time, he failed to tell the customer in advance so they could plan around the product arriving late. Everyone liked him, but he made key customers unhappy too often, created stress for the operations people, and hurt profits when key customers became frustrated and sometimes took their business to competitors. In better times we had tolerated these problems, but now his actions were creating too much internal stress and were driving away customers when we needed every order. He was clearly dysfunctional, and I had to solve this problem quickly.

The residential team was doing well. What we needed was more of their sales. I had to maximize the sales of the team and add more salespeople to increase the volume.

*Checkpoint #4: Leadership—Will our leaders handle a crisis well?* We weren't in a crisis yet, but if I didn't take action soon, we would be. If I assumed we were in the crisis and acted quickly, that would be the smartest thing to do. I remembered a rule from my SEAL days: "Plan for the worst, then anything less is easy." So if I assumed things would get worse, was I prepared?

I looked at the things crisis leaders had to do:

1. Step into the breach. I was rolling. There'd be no hiding in the office and hoping things get better. I was analyzing the problem, identifying issues, and preparing my battle plan. I'd take that plan to my people, and we'd act. I saw no problem here.
2. Clarify the problem, rally the people to action, and spark the fire. I'd been through bigger problems than this before and had gotten the job done. I could handle this part.
3. Follow through until the problem was solved. I would execute my plan until the crisis was over because I was committed to the success of this business. I wasn't going to quit, so there was no problem here.

*Checkpoint 5: Balance—Will loved ones get what they need?* My wife and I have been happily married for over thirty years and had seen tougher times than this. After talking with her and explaining that I might be a little more intense than usual, and I'd be spending more energy on work than usual, we agreed that this was not likely to be a big deal. If things went according to plan, balance would not be a problem.

The Checklist was complete. What did I learn, and what should I do? First, I had to accept that the commercial customers' needs had changed, and we hadn't responded adequately. We needed to reduce costs so we could reduce prices in order to maintain market share and minimize margin loss. Second, the residential market continued stable, and we could grow there. We needed to increase residential sales from our existing salespeople and add more sales staff to that team in order to maximize those margin dollars. And third, the dysfunctional commercial salesman was hurting us. We needed to fix the problem fast or replace him.

Without The Checklist I could have decided to focus on many other things. We could have worked to refine our financial statements, hoping that better numbers would produce different conclusions. We could have focused on pounding all our suppliers for lower material costs, hoping that by taking a pound of flesh from them we could fix our eroding commercial margins. Or we could have made plans for layoffs to reduce overhead and minimize the damage of the eroding commercial market.

Each of these actions would produce some benefit and keep us busy, but they wouldn't help us get a grip on the situation and get out of trouble. Completing any of them perfectly wouldn't produce the results that the three actions from The Checklist would produce. Though I knew what had to be accomplished, getting it done wasn't going to be easy. But if I fixed the problems, I'd be doing the right thing.

We got the job done by doing the following:

To reduce commercial product costs, we began outsourcing all items that cost us more to produce internally than they would cost if we bought them outside. We simplified product designs we had been using for many years, preserving the function of our products, but spending less labor to make them. And we eliminated some services that we had been providing free to customers that they didn't really value. The net result was that we were able to reduce costs, reduce prices, and maintain market share at acceptable margins.

To increase residential sales, we did two things. First, we focused all residential salespeople on selling our highest margin products and eliminated their involvement in selling lower margin products. The result: They sold more of the high margin products.

Second, we increased residential selling capacity by adding new salespeople and diverting some commercial salespeople's time away from low margin accounts to selling residential accounts. The result: We increased high margin residential sales.

I met with the dysfunctional salesman, and we had a plain language talk about the customer dissatisfaction, employee stress, and adverse financial impact of his actions. He said he understood and would work on improving. After a week, he had not changed his behavior, so I had the same talk with him again but told him that we could not allow the problems to continue. A week later he resigned. We found a replacement who sold more good business in his first six months than the other gentleman had in the past year. Result: Commercial sales were stronger without the dysfunctional salesman than they were with him.

It took less than one-half hour to identify the big issues using The Checklist. Once those problems were defined, it took us a few days to figure out the action plan. Though the plan didn't solve all our company's problems, it fixed the biggest ones. We survived the cash flow problem and were back on the road to financial stability.

## CHARITABLE ORGANIZATION IS STRUGGLING

I was on the board of a non-profit that had served young adults for decades, giving them outdoor learning experiences that often improved their lives dramatically. As a board, we believed that good things came from what we were doing, but course enrollments were declining and budget deficits followed. After attending a series of meetings where we struggled with "What should we do?" I took some time and went through my Checklist. Here's what I learned:

*Checkpoint #1: Commitment—Is the commitment level strong enough?* Taking a hard look at the management team, I questioned the commitment of the Executive Director. He had been in the job for many years, had been through many battles, and had recently requested a leave of absence for some personal time. Now, when the program was in trouble, he wasn't engaged. His subordinate staff included many devoted people, but some were just putting in their time because the Executive Director wasn't requiring anything more than that. The commitment of the Executive Director and its consequences was an issue that needed attention.

*Checkpoint #2: Vision—Is the vision a clear winner?* Our customers were young adults who were seeking a growth experience either because they wanted it or because their parents or a social service organization were requiring it.

First, "Who are our customers?" In simplest terms, we had three customer groups: Children of people with means, children of social service systems, and scholarship students who were children of people with limited means. The first group paid the full course fee; the second group paid negotiated fees, and the third group paid greatly reduced fees. Because part of our issue was insufficient projected income to cover budgeted program costs, it made sense to consider restructuring fees as part of our plan.

Second, "What do they value most?" In addition to expectations that the courses would be safe, all three groups expected outdoor experiential learning that would help them see the world in a way that made them function better and live more happily. They wanted this experience in the shortest time possible, because the students had other things to do with their time. And they wanted it at low cost. These expectations seemed stable, so there was no issue.

Third, "How do we provide the service in a differentiated way?" We had a beautiful outdoor setting, but so did other similar programs. We had a capable and energetic staff that loved working with the young people, but so did our competitors. We had a rich tradition of success with our students, but success stories abounded in the other programs as well. If we didn't figure out some differentiating concept, how would we present ourselves in a unique and attractive way? Improving our differentiation was a problem that needed a solution.

Fourth, "How will we sustain our organization?" With declining enrollments and a budget crisis, this was a big issue. Money came from two sources—donor contributions and course tuitions. If we continued to serve fewer students, the pool of alumni who could donate would shrink. And if enrollment continued to drop, course fees would diminish. We had to figure out how to increase enrollment, to increase course fees, and generate future donations from satisfied students and their parents.

*Checkpoint #3: People—Is the team a clear winner?* When I asked myself who was dysfunctional, the Executive Director's name came to me instantly. This was painful because he was a wonderful man. For decades he had devoted himself primarily to helping others, and as a result he lived modestly with financial reserves that wouldn't carry him very far into the future if he lost his job. But despite these personal considerations, he was in charge, and under his leadership the past several years had produced the problems we faced. Applying the Dysfunctional Person Test: Customer satisfaction—he was deficient because, though the customers liked him, he wasn't available frequently enough. Employee effectiveness and morale—he was deficient because he wasn't leading his people effectively, and they knew it. Sustaining the business and profit—he was hurting profits because of his failure to lead well. Summary: He was dysfunctional in his role as the leader.

In addition to the Executive Director, there were a few others who would probably fail the Dysfunctional Person Test, but none of them could be dealt with effectively by anyone except the Executive Director. We had to resolve the Executive Director issue in order to fix problems with him and those who reported to him.

*Checkpoint #4: Leadership—Will the leader handle a crisis well?* We were in a crisis that demanded leadership, but the Executive Director had just requested a leave of absence. What's wrong with this picture? The problem became obvious after reviewing the list of what effective crisis leaders must do:

First, assume a visible leadership position. He wasn't even there! This was a problem. Second, define the problem clearly and offer a solution everyone can attach to emotionally. He wasn't available now, so he couldn't define the problem and articulate a vision for the staff or the Board. And he hadn't done it during the past year when the problem was escalating. Third, spark a fire to energize and rally the troops to execute the plan. There was no plan, and there was no spark. Fourth, follow through until completion. He hadn't started much less followed through.

*Checkpoint #5: Balance—Will loved ones get what they need?* After a little reflection there appeared to be a balance problem in reverse. The Executive Director was focusing on his personal needs so much that he didn't have the energy or time to solve the organization's problems.

Completing the Checklist didn't take much time. The problems were clear. When I met with several board members and explained my assessment, they were relieved to have someone offer a concise picture of what was happening. But they were unhappy because the analysis led to some tough questions. Despite the discomfort, a series of meetings produced the following action plan based upon The Checklist:

- We would meet with the Executive Director to talk plainly and candidly about his responsibilities and how he was performing. These were not "take him to the woodshed" meetings; they were honest discussions to get his perspective.
- We would review the course offering to determine if we could offer shorter courses that would provide the same perceived benefits to our students. If we were successful, we would be able to offer shorter courses to make the courses attractive to more students who had limited time available; serve more students

through the existing physical facility; and reduce instructor cost per student because the same instructor wages could be spread over more students.

+ We would review our course fee structure to raise it modestly at each level. Full fee students would see a modest increase. Institutional programs would receive smaller discounts. And we would create a special sponsor program, allowing donors to support specific needy children.

+ We decided to expand our revenue base by having staff present our program to social service organizations that served needy children but had no current relationship with us.

+ We would describe our new plan to large donors and ask for a one-time special donation to help us bridge the gap to implementation of our plan.

The plan worked. The Executive Director admitted he was tired and just couldn't face the organization's challenges. He said he had been considering alternative ways to serve youth that didn't involve the complex administrative responsibilities of his current job. We arranged an extension of his leave, and he found a job doing what he loved most.

Soon we found a new Executive Director who willingly accepted our analysis and plan. He assembled a capable team, and through his energetic efforts the course offerings were revised and expanded, enrollments began increasing, donors provided transitional support, and the organization reached new levels of service to youth and financial stability within two years.

# CHAPTER NINE

# Avoiding Burnout

So you've followed the Checklist and achieved amazing results. Congratulations! You've earned your success. But how long can you continue to perform well? What will keep you charged with energy while others burn out?

To answer these questions, consider the following people who seem to love what they do. What do they have in common that keeps them going strong?

*Scenario 1: A classic example is Mother Theresa. This woman lived with poor people under adverse physical conditions for decades. She had continuous opportunities to live a safer, more comfortable life but she chose not to. Why?*

*Scenario 2: Two friends of ours are married and work together. They routinely put in sixty-hour weeks and say they love their work. They've become financially secure through their efforts, so why do they continue the long hours?*

As we think about people who work energetically for many years and don't yearn for retirement, what images emerge? I see many clergy, some teachers, some nurses, some craftsmen, some coaches, and a few business people. As I've asked these people why they continue to work, I hear two basic answers: Some need the money, but most of them simply love what they do. And among those who love what they do, what is it that they love? The most common answer contains some form of the statement, "I like helping the people we serve."

> Charlie was a woodworker. He loved making furniture for people. It made him feel good when someone came to his shop, described the piece they wanted, and then smiled when he brought it to them. He didn't need the money, but he continued making beautiful woodwork for people long after his friends had retired.

These people feel that they are doing something beneficial for others, and they like that feeling…so they want to keep working. If we believe that everyone ultimately does what's in their personal best interest, these people value the good feelings from serving others enough that their commitment to work remains high.

If burnout candidates felt that they were doing something

for others, rather than just working for a paycheck or other very practical reasons, maybe they would change their minds, enjoy their work more, and choose to continue working rather than fighting burnout. But how can that happen?

## BELIEVE THAT YOU ARE DOING SOMETHING BENEFICIAL FOR THOSE YOU SERVE

Someone is buying your products or using your services. Your product or service is valuable to them or they wouldn't be buying it. Feel good about that.

> As a young commercial banker much of my work was boring, and the paper pushing was endless. But when I analyzed opportunities with clients and provided financing that created jobs and developed products, I felt a real sense of satisfaction. We were doing something that benefited many people, and that reality felt good. By concentrating on those good feelings, I stayed at the job several years longer than if my only concern had been the size of my paycheck.

**"THERE IS NOTHING BETTER FOR A MAN OR WOMAN THAN THAT THEY SHOULD EAT AND DRINK, AND FIND ENJOYMENT IN THEIR WORK."**
—Ecclesiastes 2:24

If you and your team connect with that sense of providing value to others, good feelings naturally follow.

> In the SEAL Teams we worked long hours doing dangerous

*activities in constant physical discomfort, separated from our families more than half of each year and for lower wages than our civilian counterparts. Why? Some of us liked the lifestyle. But many of us, including Hershel, also felt that we were protecting a way of life for our families, friends, and all Americans. We believed that our missions would make the world a safer place, so the sacrifices were worthwhile.*

## BELIEVE THAT YOU ARE DOING SOMETHING BENEFICIAL FOR YOUR PEOPLE

How many people feel that their bosses really care about them? How many people feel valued in their workday life? How many people feel their incomes are secure because their organization is strong? Too many people don't have good feelings about these questions.

If you lead your team well enough that your organization is stable, and if decisions that affect your people come from caring and supportive intentions, you create a healthy environment. Many people don't have that; everyone wants that. If you are providing it, you are doing a good thing. Recognize that and feel good about it.

*Pete was viewed as a tough manager because he expected everyone to do their fair share and didn't tolerate those* who wouldn't, but his people were loyal to him and stayed with him. Taking care of customers was his top priority because they paid the bills. Taking care of his people was his second priority because they took care of his customers.

He knew all of his customers and employees by name, and he knew many of their spouses. When any of his good people had a serious personal problem, he wanted to know about it. He couldn't help with every problem, but helped when he could. He provided a valuable service to his customers and was proud of it. His people had stable incomes, a clean and healthy work environment, and regular recognition for doing good work. He felt good about that, too. Pete focused on the good things and continued his work for many years after friends had burned out or retired.

# AFTERWORD

There's no place like America. If you've traveled abroad, you understand how wonderful our country is. America is not perfect, but there's a big gap between what we have and second place. Our currency is stable and is the standard for the world. Our stock exchanges generate capital for most of the world's major business. Our English is the international language of air travel. Our technology is the most copied in the world. Our democratic system of government inspires revolutionary action by oppressed peoples. And our free market system is the model for emerging economies. No other nation in the modern world can truthfully make these statements.

Because we have both freedom and a stable environment, we Americans enjoy unmatched opportunities to create what we want to create. But opportunity is always linked to risk, and risk is linked to tough decisions. So, to take the fullest advantage of our freedom, you have to be brave and make smart decisions.

Periodically, you will reach those moments when the fullness of the American opportunity is available to you. All that will stand between you and success will be action based on good decisions. It is a frightening and wonderful experience all wrapped up on one!

That's the time to use The Checklist and be brave. Checklists based upon wisdom from successful past experience reduce mistakes, and courage trumps the fear you will feel. If you use The Checklist, muster enough courage, and add a little luck, you'll succeed.

God blessed America…now it's up to you.

# ABOUT THE AUTHOR

Alan R. Horner has been successfully improving mid-size businesses and non-profits for thirty years. He has a perfect win/loss record of leading turnarounds in manufacturing, wholesaling, retailing, service, and construction businesses as well as several non-profit organizations. In the process he has saved the jobs of many people, but more importantly he has improved the quality of life for those whose jobs he saved and has developed a cadre of leaders among his subordinates.

The lessons in *Get A Grip* are not theoretical concepts—they are the practical fruit of several decades' of real-world success. The Checklist questions and The Pearls are brought to life through anecdotes about the people who touched his life and made each element of the book real.

After graduating from the University of Wisconsin with a B.A. in Biology, Mr. Horner became an officer in the SEAL/UDT Teams during the Vietnam era. The key elements of his Checklist were formulated during those incredibly challenging years when he led the SEAL/UDT parachute team and also led the first combat mini-sub group in the East Coast SEAL Teams. After the navy he began his business career while simultaneously earning an

MBA with academic honors from the University of Minnesota.

In the mid-1980s he was invited to join the prestigious Young President's Organization (YPO) and subsequently joined the World President's Organization (WPO). His years in these organizations brought him insights and access that, in combination with his daily activities, allowed him to refine his Checklist, making it more succinct and effective.

To contact the author or learn more about services available to individuals or organizations based on the material in Get a Grip, go to:

www.getagripusa.net

or www.bronzebowpublishing.com

# QUICK REFERENCE FOR GET A GRIP

| THE CHECKLIST QUESTIONS |
| --- |

Checkpoint **❶** : Is my/our commitment level strong enough?
- Time
- Money
- Emotional energy

Checkpoint **❷** : Is my/our vision a clear winner?
- Who are the customers?
- What do they value most?
- How do we provide differentiated value?
- How do we sustain ourselves?

Checkpoint **❸** : Is the team a clear winner?

Checkpoint **❹** : Will the leaders handle crises well?

Checkpoint **❺** : Will my loved ones get what they need?

| THE DYSFUNCTIONAL PERSON TEST |
| --- |

**❶** Is this person hurting customer satisfaction?

**❷** Is this person hurting good teammates?

**❸** Is this person hurting profits?

## THE PEARLS

**Pearl #1:** The 7 P's: Proper Prior Planning Prevents Pathetically Poor Performance.

**Pearl #2:** Whoever Gives Up First Loses.

**Pearl #3:** Every Sale Starts With Listening.

**Pearl #4:** If It's a Winner, Pump It. If It's a Loser, Dump It.

**Pearl #5:** Your Plan Will Be Wrong Tomorrow.

**Pearl #6:** Hire Slow and Fire Fast.

**Pearl #7:** True Champions Don't Win Just Once; They Win Year After Year.


## ESSENTIAL ACTIONS OF A CRISIS LEADER

**❶** Takes control visibly and immediately.

**❷** Defines the challenge simply and creates a vision for action that people attach to emotionally.

**❸** Emits energy that sparks exceptional performance.

**❹** Follows through, completing critical tasks, until the problem is solved.